CO-CREATION: MYSTERY SOLVED!

Author's website: www.filibertoamati.com

Cover image: creative idea: Francisco Pestana; main picture "Flipster holding Poster" © Peshkova, license acquired on 6/5/2014 on Dreamstime.com; cover graphics: Filiberto Amati.

All other internal images belong to Filiberto Amati, except: "Group of friends taking picture with mobile phone" © Goodluz (Stock Photo ID: 16991051, bigstockphoto.com); "Mountain lake in National Park High Tatra" © Leonid Tit (Stock Photo ID: 43915993, bigstockphoto.com); "Starlings" © Digoarpi (Stock Photo ID: 7041756, bigstockphoto.com); "Couple of modern young people posing on a road over picturesque landscape" © prometeus (Stock Photo ID: 42658690, bigstockphoto.com); "Creative team working together in a modern office" © Wavebreak Media Ltd (Stock Photo ID: 46875367, bigstockphoto.com);

ISBN-13: 978-1502776877
ISBN-10: 1502776871

Table of Contents

60

67

IV

EXAMPLES

CONCLUSIONS

ANNEX

INTRODUCTION

The main objective of this guide is to create and, at the same time, to structure my experiences and my memories of co-creation over the past fifteen years. By doing so, I also hope to be able to provide insight and, in some cases, answers to the many questions about co-creation that customers, friends and family usually ask me. The goal is not, however, to provide all the of answers. Instead, I would like to help readers formulate key questions which will allow them to enter the world of co-creation on their own terms. In fact, as so often happens in the world of innovation and marketing, there are no absolute rights or wrongs. Instead, there are answers, which are appropriate in the convergence of external and internal factors related to a particular enterprise. Therefore, it is not the objective of this script to provide 'the' answer to each question, but, instead, to hint at how we can formulate the appropriate and necessary questions to fully understand co-creation.

Special thanks go to Hollis Kurman, who introduced me to the world of co-creation during my experience at her Dutch consulting boutique. A special thanks also go to my father, Aldo Piero Amati, who, with persistence and patience, helped me in cleaning up the original Italian version of this book. Sadly, he passed away one week before we received the first batch of books from the press.

Finally, I would like to mention Francisco Pestana and Xavier Lesauvage, with whom I literally co-created from New York to Moscow.

CO-CREATION: BACKGROUND

At the dawn of co-creation, the search for new methods of synergy and collaboration between consumers and end-users in the manufacturing of products or provision of services began. Already in 1979, scholars such as Lovelock and Young had emphasized the importance of consumers and how they could increase the productivity level of a company. Early emphasis was placed on manufacturing operations. In fact, years later, we began to refer to this particular process as 'co-production', and it remains quite distinct from the concepts of product development, innovation and marketing. The debate on the merits of co-production continued until the end of the 1990's. Professionals, researchers and executives ad-dressed and debated this particular theory in specialized magazines and everyday practice, evaluating the benefits and risks of increasing con-sumer and customer involvement in the production process.

By 1993, several eminent scholars had begun pointing to inherent limita-tions within the theory of 'co-production', as well as what they perceived to be inevitable conclusions of the process, largely the use of customers and consumers merely to reduce costs and increase productivity. Adams

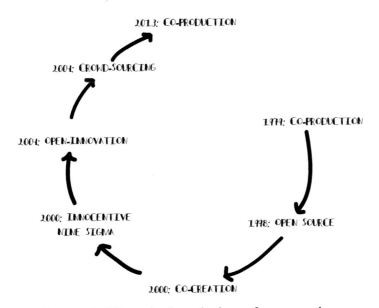

Image 1. Historical evolution of co-creation

and Song, however, claim that consumers can be used to develop new methods of differentiating products and services within a given target market, ultimately allow for a long-lasting, competitive advantage over rival businesses. More intensive discussions on the concept of 'co-creation' did not began until the arrival of the 21st century. In 2000, Prahalad and Ramaswamy, under the impressive mantle of the Harvard Business Review, introduced the concept of co-creation.

The world they describe is composed of customers and producers who create value for each other, while, simultaneously, remaining in competition with one another. Customers take an active role in shaping their own experience, as well as in educating, generating expectations and developing a solid, powerful foundation for a brand or product in the marketplace. Central to the vision of Prahalad and Ramaswamy is the large role that digital technologies play in promoting a sense of community between brand owners and consumers purchasing products from the brand in question. Essentially, the contents of brand communication

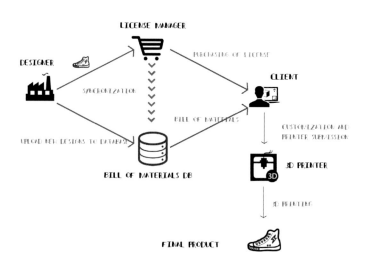

Image 2. Example of co-production ecosystem

are no longer exclusively produced by a company's marketing department, but are instead located anywhere within the consumer / customer ecosystem. Since the year 2000, more than twenty-thousand books, articles and research papers have been published in English on the topic of co-creation. In the year 2013 alone, approximately three thousand publications referenced the idea of co-creation and its potential impact on innovation, brand development, advertising, content marketing and design, and a variety of other topics. It is, therefore, crucial to pause for a moment and reflect on the evolution of the concept of co-creation, from the theory originally presented in 2000 and the more complicated, sometimes radical, and too often, generalized definition, which exists today. Metaphorically speaking, co-creation is now thought of as a great metropolis, where ideas can meet and sub- cultures can collide, including wealth, poverty, sustainability, natural resource waste, political and religious ideology, as well as rational and irrational logics.

Continuing along the lines of the metaphor of the metropolis, each of these ideas share common features, but they also have that certain 'je ne se quoi' which makes them unique and helps them to stand out from others. The same can be said for co-creation. As for the future paradigm, it is plausible to assume that technological innovation will help sustain and nourish the concepts and the phenomenon of co-production ("Image 1. Historical evolution of co-creation" on page 4). With the rapid evolution of three-dimensional printing and the giant steps being taken in nanotechnology, famous scholars and many field experts expect that in the near future, for many categories, a significant element of the production process will be controlled by consumers. This near future will be characterized by ecosystems ("Image 2. Example of co-production ecosystem" on page 5) in which a consumer can buy a design of a 3D object, purchase a brand license, and, through the use of specific software applications, personalize the branded product before producing it using a personal or specialized 3D printer. In the following chapter, we will examine a definition for co-creation, with the caveat that with the increasing number of researchers, managers and consultants that make co-creation their "daily bread", it is almost impossible to give a single comprehensive overview of the concept. Our definition represents a specific perspective on co-creation, based on the knowledge and experience of the writer and his collaborators.

DEFINITION AND ANTI-DEFINITION

Providing a clear a definition is a difficult task and often, when discussing the topic with clients, colleagues and scholars, we found that there is much easier way of gaining insight into how these individuals understand and explain this topic. Instead of focusing on the "definition" of co-creation, we opted instead to offer our interviewees the option to develop an 'anti-definition'. In a nutshell, by asking them which elements their definition does not include, we aim at understanding what it truly "is". In this chapter we will examine a definition and an 'anti-definition' of co-creation, just to make sure everyone is on the same page.

CO—CREATION: A DEFINITION

From a semantic point of view, the word co-creation carries the following meaning:

> *"An act of invention, produced by a diverse group of actors."*

Putting aside social sciences and psychology, and, instead, focusing on a business-related view of this definition, there are four dimensions that

Image 3. Definition of co-creation

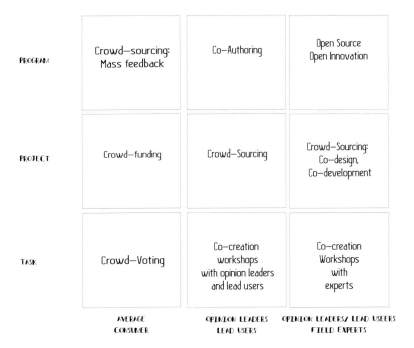

	AVERAGE CONSUMER	OPINION LEADERS LEAD USERS	OPINION LEADERS/ LEAD USEERS FIELD EXPERTS
PROGRAM	Crowd—sourcing: Mass feedback	Co—Authoring	Open Source Open Innovation
PROJECT	Crowd—funding	Crowd—Sourcing	Crowd—Sourcing: Co—design, Co—development
TASK	Crowd—Voting	Co—creation workshops with opinion leaders and lead users	Co—creation Workshops with experts

Image 4. Types of co-creation

can be derived ("Image 3. Definition of co-creation" on page 9):

- **Actors**: those who are actively involved in the process. The actors in co-creation are not only stakeholders within the company, but also suppliers, customers, consumers and external experts. The presence of both internal and external partners is a key element of the process of co-development, and it is often where our definition ceases to overlap with many already in existence.

- **Action**: this dimensiont includes different typologies of actions, such as designing a new object, improving an existing product, or defining the main characteristics for the launch or re-launch of a brand in the relevant marketplace. Obviously, these actions do not exist in an organizational vacuum, and therefore require derivative, related and equally critical tasks, such as planning, coordination and control. It's important to note that derivative actions do not, in themselves, constitute co-creative actions.

- **Object**: in a business context, the content which is the subject of co-creation may refer to a product, service, brand, business model, business process or organizational tool.

- **Mode**: on-line, off-line and mixed.

The most classic and extreme case of co-creation exists in the world of software and digital content. Firefox (as well as all of Mozilla's products) and Wikipedia products are commonly referred to as "open source" and "open content" models. In an open source model1, source code is freely available, while open content models typically allow for free distribution of content (even under license type Creative Commons). The goal of both of these platforms is to further the evolution of the product or content in question through the effort and the collaboration of multiple actors. The cases are extreme because they are continuous in time and feature multi-dimensional development. Another example of co-creation is that of the French company Danone. Danone creates partnerships involving co-creation, co-design and co-financing with non-governmental organizations, institutions, foundations, research centers and social entrepreneurs, the goal being to provide joint responses to the problems of the poorest sectors of the world's population, while simultaneously developing ideas, products and services that improve living conditions in the same areas. There are also a variety of other specific instances of co-creation, where marketing and product development departments meet in creative workshops with consumers and experts, with the goal of solving a specific problem or generating new ideas. Many multinational firms involved in fast-moving goods and consumer electronics embark on these types of projects with the aim of validating or improving existing concepts or to generate new ideas. In order to provide further examples of co-creation, it is necessary to begin to provide taxonomy of co-creation itself. This will also allow us to identify the elements that are typically included in the general definition of co-creation which may have nothing to do with the examples outlined above. To do this, we will consider two dimensions, as seen in "Image 4. Types of co-creation" on page 10. The first is that of external actors, or people not employed by the company, that are involved in co-creation. Within this subject, we will create the following three categories:

- **Mainstream Consumers**: all consumers within a diffusion model who are neither innovators nor early adopters.
- **Opinion Leaders/ Lead-users**: those individuals who are not only aware of current trends, but are also able to spread an idea using their social networks.

- **Experts**: this category includes both experts in a specific field, such as industrial designers, architects, creative communications, etc., as well as opinion leaders, best thought of as consumers who have specific experience in a field, such as art, music, narrative, or large-scale distribution and the marketing.

The second dimension of the model is *the type of involvement of external resources*. This can include:

- **Tasks**: here defined as punctual and occasional activities, which are individualized and not interconnected among themselves. They include workshops, online forums, surveys, etc...

- **Project**: a set of multiple tasks, all of which feature a single, well-defined objective. These occur during a period of medium duration, which can range from a few weeks to a few months.
- **Program**: a set of multiple projects which form a clear strategy and a long-term partnership, typically measured in years.

From the intersection of these dimensions, we can derive nine combinations, each featuring a specific methodology of co-creation:

1. **Crowd-voting**: one of the unwritten rules of online communities is the formula known as '1/9/90': One percent of the population creates new concepts or generates new ideas, nine percent helps to filter and promote them, and 90% has little or no involvement. Crowd-voting is the element of co-creation which involves the nine percent, as this group is asked to help evaluate the potential of co-generated ideas.

2. **Co-creation Workshops with leading edge consumers**: this includes creative exercises lasting one or more days, in which a small group of consumers, opinion leaders and managers of a company work together to solve a problem or generate ideas that effectively tap into a new market opportunity. These workshops are useful for generating a deeper understanding of brand adoption dynamics and product categories, as well as to measure the effectiveness of a new prototype or concept.

3. **Co-creation Workshops with experts**: this concept is similar to the previous idea, but involves consumer experts or field experts. For example, in situations where a new product was being launched, an expert in modern trade would be used. If, for example, a new category of lighting products were being developed, an architect

would be consulted. This approach is useful in situations where international expansion is likely.

4. **Crowd-funding**: platforms that allow for fundraising to support a new, innovative product, or the gathering of financial resources for commercialization purposes. Fundraising can be in the form of a loan, a donation, purchase of the first production run or purchasing shares in the company: each of the above situations have in common the peer-to-peer relationship between donor and recipient, and the presence of an intermediary who is the guarantor of the transaction from both sides. Although these factors are typically included in the co-creation process, we shall see later on that, in reality, they do not necessarily belong to our definition. Among the most well known platforms are Kiva, Kickstarter and Indiegogo.

5. **Crowd-sourcing/ Delegation of decisions**: this is quite typical in the development of communication, design-related or creative projects in general. One of the most popular examples involves the creation of a contest where the client involves a community of creative people who develop a new advertisement, new packaging, or related accessories, and then they vote for the winning solution. This segment only somewhat coincides with our definition of co-creation, primarily because the participation of the client is more typical in agency-client relationships than those involving co-creation, with the exception of the final decision, which often gets delegated to a panel of voters.

6. **Crowd-sourcing/ Co-design / Co-development**: this is perhaps one of the most interesting dimensions of co-creation. It often includes a variety of types of activities, with diverse and often complementary mechanics. Among those, one of our favorite examples is Diageo, which organized a bartenders' competition within their own educational platform, ultimately designed to help lead to the

creation of a new brand and a new product category for their reserve portfolio. The winner is expected to receive 5% of net sales during the first five years after the launch of the new brand.

7. **Crowd-sourcing/ Mass Feedback**: this segment includes elements of co-creation directly linked with market research. That being said, this typically falls outside our definition of co-creation.

8. **Co-Authoring**: one of the best examples of co-authoring is Wikipedia, the online encyclopedia, whose contents are created, validated and managed by user groups, which are organized according to a traditional hierarchy. Other examples of this system includes map sites such as OpenStreetMap and Distributed Proofreaders, the latter of which involves users who donate their time to proofread the Gutenberg Project, which has worked in the digitization and archiving of Western cultural heritage since 1971.

9. **Open Source/ Open Innovation**: this cluster contains two distinct elements that come together almost by accident, although they definitely have targets in common. We will devote a paragraph to the relationship between co-creation and open innovation later on, so here we will provide only examples of open source platforms. Two primary examples immediately come to mind, those being Linux, the open operating system of Unix type, created by Linus Torvald, and Sourceforge, an online archive for the development and management of the elaboration of open source software.

It should be noted that our definition of co-creation differs from those generally accepted by the community at large, particularly due to the fact that professionals in the world of marketing, research and development accept the delegation of decisions as part of co-creation. From our perspective, this simply does not fit into a context of mutual development, testing, validation and researching by internal company forces and external groups. By logical extension, delegating decisions also happens in television competitions, where televoting is used. Should this be considered an example of co-creation? From our humble point of view, they are just marketing tricks to increase the involvement of the audience, but do not fall within the scope of co-creation. At the same time, let us remember that in all processes related to the validation of a prototype and the creation of a new concept, or in processes that are fundamental to co-creation, screening, or selection a subset of items from a larger set, collaboration is an integral part of the process. Ergo during co-creation choices are made, but limiting the nature of selection to a contest in which the winners are chosen by other participants does not seem to be part of a process of co-development, but rather a marketing strategy designed to engage and retain final consumers.

We will enter now into the details of the relationship between open innovation and co-creation, before concluding with our 'anti-definition'.

CO–CREATION AND OPEN INNOVATION

In order to understand the concept of open innovation, we must first understand how the process of innovation has evolved in recent years. During the early years of innovation management, research and development departments were solely responsible for the creation and conception of new products. Since the company's strategies were strongly influenced by the philosophy of first-mover advantage, innovation was conceived largely as a strategic element and was accomplished internally in complete secrecy, even withheld from the company environment itself. The next development phase of the innovation management process proposed a somewhat more liberated medium. In so-called collaborative innovation, there is awareness that not all aspects of the development of new technologies can be processed internally. Strategic suppliers are gradually introduced into the development process, and collaboration becomes more open, leading to the creation of new markets and new products. One of the best examples of this collaborative model is probably found in the automotive sector, where producers involve first-level suppliers in the design of new vehicles. The third stage in the evolution of the innovation process is that of open innovation. The most compelling element of open innovation involves the development of an ecosystem where companies cooperate to exchange not only patents and licenses, but also knowledge and experience. The process of describing, describing open innovation remains somewhat elusive: in 2013, there were only 17,000 publications in the English language on the subject, which is clearly vast and complex. That being said, some studies are proving to be immensely interesting, such as a classification given by Feller that takes into account two main dimensions, through which the author identifies and classifies different components at the heart of the discipline. These dimensions are:

1. **Purpose**: typically, the companies involved in open innovation ecosystems tend to collaborate in one of two ways. The first is through patent development, while the second includes patents and product innovation. In the first case, companies exchange and acquire technological developments or create alliances designed for the exploitation of patents. An example may be that of a company that has developed internally one or more patents, which then fails to exploit it commercially. In this case, the company will then look for a partner who will purchase or license that technology, or perhaps create a joint venture for the exploitation of the same product. In the second case, the mechanism is more complex, largely because it requires not only the provision of existing technological solutions, but also the willingness to design technologies in conjunction with

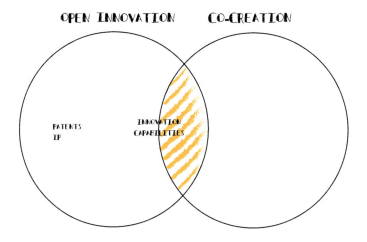

Image 5. Example overlap between OI and Co-creation

one another.

2. **Type of relation**: companies can choose to collaborate within a context of open innovation, developing a direct relationship with other companies, perhaps through brokers, in an effort to create a powerful ecosystem.

Feller then proposes four sub-segments of open innovation, resulting from various combinations of "purpose" and "relationship":

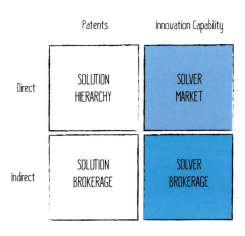

In detail, the segments are characterized in the following mannerr:

1. **Solution Hierarchy:** companies involved in this segment intend to develop direct business relationships or partnerships with external entities that allow them to exploit internally produced inventions that have not yet been put into use commercially and to have the opportunity to acquire inventions of others that makes no sense to try to replicate internally. We talk about entities involved, because often university institutions and research laboratories, which do not necessarily have profit-based motives, are often active at the same level of for-profit companies.

2. **Solver Market:** as in the previous case, the object of the transaction is typically a patent that already exists, therefore an invention that is already registered and tested. In this case, the object is less tangible because it requires support from a group or individual who has specific expertise and ability to innovate in a certain area. Basically, we look for someone with whom we can combine resources to develop the patent together, or an institution that develops inventions to solve a concrete problem.

3. **Solution Brokerage:** in this case, as in the example following this, the presence of an intermediary guarantees a more effective meeting point between the demand and

offer of patents. The role of the intermediary is critical, both on the demand side and the offer side, primarily due to the fact that this individual helps the applicant to formulate the problem in a coherent structure to help evaluate what is needed for continued research. Additionally, the intermediary ensures, through an examination of the credentials, credibility and quality of solutions and suppliers, reducing the risk of patent infringement.

4. **Solver Brokerage:** here, we are dealing with an intermediary who guarantees the credibility of the potential innovation partner. Nevertheless, the risk is slightly higher than in the previous case, due to the fact that the two partners may not be able to develop a joint solution.

The two types of open innovation referred to here involve the idea of innovative capacity and, thus, create an opportunity for two separate and distinct entities to develop a solution to a problem together, therefore fitting our definition of co-creation. At the same time, the commercial exchange of patents does not fall within our definition of co-creation, because it is based on commercial transactions of patents and licenses, which has nothing to do with the development of new ideas.

EVERYTHING CO–CREATION IS NOT...

Following the definition of co-creation that we have proposed, we derive that from the many dimensions that our explanation does include, it does not incorporate two popular phenomena, those being 'UGC', or user-generated content, as well as crowd-voting. When discussing UGC, two examples typically emerge.

The first is the Doritos campaign named "Crash the SuperBowl." A subsidiary of Pepsi's Frito-Lay, Doritos launched a campaign in 2007, which asked consumers to help them produce an advertisement for the upcoming NFL championship match. Doritos promised viewers that the selected candidate would have their ad shown during SuperBowl 2008, the most exclusive and expensive television event in the entire United States. Nearly two thousand ads participated in the competition, and the piece which received the most votes was transmitted during one of the commercial breaks of the event, thus leaving control of the advertising campaign and of promotions related to the event in the hands of the consumers.

The second example is a campaign launched by Tourism of Queensland, Australia, which was unable to afford large investments to promote tourism to the Great Barrier Reef. The department created a clever campaign which quickly went viral due to how well it resonated with the global community. At the center of the campaign is a job offer as guardian of an island in the region, with 65.000 dollars paid for six months, plus food and housing. The duties involved included taking care of the fish, cleaning the pool and maintain a blog on the island. To be able to apply to what was promoted as the "Best Job in the World", individuals simply had to create a promotional video, detailing why he or she was the ideal candidate. To choose the candidate, online visitors voted as to which video they thought was best Approximately thirty-five thousand candidates from around the world applied, leading to more than four million visits to the website of Tourism of Queensland. Overall, more than six-thousands stories were published about this particular campaign while it was running. In both of these examples, it appears that the role of the company and of consumers is not based on dialectic. In fact, in each case, the company's role is to provide a platform for participants to develop and create, regardless of the contents of their particular product, which are then used by the company for their own media platform.

Both are competitions, involving the delegation of creation to the participants, as well as the choice of the winner to an election among the participants themselves. These contests, although heterogeneous, do not provide any direct interaction between the main actors or the company. Consumers and experts do not participate in work sessions to jointly solve a problem or create a new product, service or brand, or to take advantage of a new market opportunity. In fact, they are not much different from competitions related to the purchase of a product, which creates an opportunity for participants to win a prize.

By virtue of the same principle, crowd-funding, which is considered one of the synonyms of co-creation, does not fall within our definition. This is because the concept, including the brand and the product, are developed by independent creators, without the help of external actors. The latter have an important role, because they help an idea or product reach the market, but do not offer any technical support, except when they serve as a sounding board during the developmental phase. Obviously, crowd-funding platforms play an epochal and innovative role, allowing many dreams locked in the drawer to be manufactured and marketed in a context in which the industry value chain, to which they belong, would not allow their launch. Despite this, the encounter between demand and supply of external financing does not fall within our definition of co-creation

CO-CREATING: WITH WHOM?

As we have seen in previous chapters, the process of co-creation can occur with different types of actors, whether they are mass consumers, opinion leaders, consumer ex-perts or authorities in the field. In this chapter we propose, based on our experience, a point of view directly related to the type of consumer that is best designed for involvement in the process of co-creation. For this purpose, we introduce three basic concepts: homophily, complex adaptive systems, and swarm intelligence. Each of these concepts allows us, with some degree of authority, to support the following hypothesis: co-creation with opinion leaders and experts allows you to develop creative and relevant solutions, while simultaneously allowing you to create ideas that can, in the future, enjoy massive development.

HOMOPHILY

The principle of homophily is a concept of which we are instinctually aware, but perhaps unconsciously. In Italian popular folklore, it is reflected in the expression, "God makes them, and then pair them" and "wives and oxen from your town." In English, it is customary to refer to the same concept with the phrase, "Birds of feather flock together." At the basis of the idea is the realization that our social connections, like those of many animal species, rely on similarity. Our social networks tend to be homogenous in terms of socio-demographic, geographic, behavioral and interpersonal characteristics. Of course, this does not mean that there are no relations with individuals who do not fall into certain categories, but the probability that these heterophilic relationships will dissolve over time is higher than in homophilic relationships. Of course, these relationships are complicated and change over time. Social networks allow you to keep in touch with people who are physically distant, and this creates a considerable level of complexity that scholars and researchers around the world are researching intently. However, from our point of view, it also explains how certain consumption choices of individuals can be traced to the need to normalize homophilic relations. The consumption of a product or a brand, in many cases, is not the goal, but the need that an individual has for integration within a group, i.e "consume ergo belong."

COMPLEX ADAPTIVE SYSTEMS

Complex adaptive systems are sophisticated ecosystems formed by groups of homogeneous individuals, each group forming a system, which is heterogeneous from the other. These systems are complex because they tend to adapt to changes in the ecosystem of the other groups, although their survival conditions are not at risk. They can also adapt to changes within the ecosystem, but outside of their group, according to a logic that is neither individual nor of the team, but of the system. For example, let's examine a small lake, with a variety of plants and wildlife. Each species represents a group or a homogeneous system, but each is heterogeneous relative to the other systems. There are models – although unrelated to our current discourse - explaining, for example, how to change the behavior of fish, and the changing role of different groups of underwater flora relative to the fluctuations in the fish. What interests us is the presence of a dynamic equilibrium between distinct

groups within an ecosystem.

SWARM INTELLIGENCE

The theory of "swarm intelligence", is a complex concept, although we will try to introduce it in a simplified form, suited directly for our purposes. Given a large number of like-minded individuals who are capable of acting independently, all of whom are more or less sophisticated, swarm intelligence can commonly be thought of as the process by which generalizations are created to predict or model intelligent behavior of a group at large. A typical example, which gives its name to the phenomenon in Italian, is a swarm of birds, which tends to behave as if the individuals who compose it were guided by a common understanding and common choices of the group.

This principle makes it possible to better understand the phenomena of "word of mouth" and the adoption of technological innovation: consumer groups who are not adept to change, perhaps are even afraid, ultimately follow larger trends due to the presence of group intelligence that goes beyond the needs of individuals. This also explains why in popular folklore, some justify behavior with the phrase, "But everybody does it."

OPINION LEADERS AND EXPERTS

Summing up the three concepts above, we can conclude that: Individual choices are often motivated by the need to belong to a group; group behaviors often occur as a result of adapting to new behaviors of heterogeneous groups, though belonging to the same ecosystem; individual behaviors are guided by an intelligence group, but not necessarily by  individual choices. The first conclusion implies that in order to effectively develop a product that is adopted by a class of consumers, it is important to try to please those who create the rules of the group or who may be able to introduce innovations in rituals of communication and belonging. Who better than the opinion leaders of the group? Who better than brand experts, who have the trust of the group to be able to change the character of consumption and communication?

The second conclusion tells us that there are trends for specific segments of consumers who are capable of changing the balance of the market. Consumers who have not immediately adopted certain trends, or who are not part of a larger group, may end up changing their behavior because of the actions of the majority. Therefore, if our goal is to change the rules of the game in a market, who better than trend-setters and opinion leaders to introduce an innovation, a new brand or a new business model? The third conclusion implies that even the most secularized choices should reflect the interests of consumer groups in order to limit fluctuations caused by the influence of the majority. It is better to focus on the intelligence of the group rather than the individual. What decisions are likely to appeal to those who are used to shaping the opinion of the group and shaping group logic?

Co-creating with opinion leaders and experts allows you to develop solutions that are relevant to them. They can not only change the rules of the groups to which they belong, but also change the consumption habits of other segments within the same 'ecosystem'. So the leaders of opinion are, based on our experience, the most suitable class of consumers to participate in a co-creation. They tend to be more creative than the average population, they are definitely more informed, and are aware of current trends. They are also the most direct and effective communicators, which makes them much more efficient in co-creation, and may represent an incredible source of inspiration. Obviously, opinion leaders are not individuals with absolute knowledge: an opinion leader in cameras, for example, is not necessarily informed of what is happening in the world of spirits, just as a trend-setter in sportswear is not necessarily aware of the trends in the world of makeup or hair treatments. Also, in keeping with what was discussed when presenting the concept of homophile, opinion leaders tend to be those within a specific demographic segment and may not be perfectly matched for the entire population.

CO-CREATING: HOW MANY?

Very often, co-creation enters into a business context through the door of market research. Even intuitively, it is not difficult to understand why projects that deal with different types of consumers are primarily managed by those who make sure to listen to customers and end-users. In the world of market research, there is a separation between qualitative research and quantitative analysis. It is best interpreted using two dimensions, inversely proportional to each other, as well as the available knowledge concerning risk. In qualitative investigations, it is possible to ask many questions to participants, primarily through the use of audio and visual metaphors, which grasp deeper motivations from both the conscious and the unconscious mind. These qualitative research methods also allow the formulation of hypotheses concerning the definition of the main themes of the research. However, this could be risky as they do not represent a sample of the population that is large enough to be meaningful. That is, useful for formulating hypotheses, not enough to reach solid conclusions and representative of a larger group of consumers. On the other hand, a quantitative survey can provide clearer conclusions on the market potential of an idea, although it does not allow researchers to draw clear and unambiguous lines between causes and effects. By virtue of the affinity of co-creation with market research, and the relationship between quality and quantity in investigations of consumption, it is clear that this has led to the formation of one of the great urban legends about co-creation: co-creating with many participants reduces risks, and therefore, the object of the process of co-development is more significant in relevant markets.

It should be noted, before proceeding further, that co-creation with dozens, if not hundreds of people at a time is almost exclusively reserved for internet platforms and social networks. This could include discussion forums, chat, and interactions on Facebook, Twitter and LinkedIn. In the next chapter, we will discuss in more detail the benefits of co-creation online rather than face-to-face meetings in which the participants are physically in the same place. It is important to remember that co-creation is a team effort, and that the final result depends not only on the quality of each individual participant's effort, but also on the diversity of the group and the relationships that are created within the group.

Then, we will examine the dynamics of various working groups, starting from a generally accepted model. For those who, like the writer, have had the pleasure of being a student of IESE Prof. Paddy Miller, an example leaps to mind based on the 1957 film of Henry Fonda titled '12 Angry men'. The film tells the story of a juror, played by Henry Fonda, who attempts to persuade the other eleven members of the jury to acquit the accused. The film is a great tool for understanding the dynamics within a

NAME	ROLE
Teamworkers	Keep the group together
Specialist	Provide knowledge and expertise in their field
Resource Investigator	Play the "Devil's Advocate"
Coordinator	Provide focus to the team
Shapers	Provide motivation to the team
Coimpleter Finisher	Finalize the work
Plant	Creativity and problem solving
Implementers	Develop a strategic plan
Monitor Evaluator	Provide objectivity to the group

Image 6. Types of roles in a group

group, and how those who have a minority opinion can convince others to change their voting intention. In fact, the film is an excellent tool for displaying the concepts outlined by Prof. Belbin concerning group behavior, as well as the theory of the latter on the dynamics and optimization of the same. Belbin discusses a variety of ways that we assume roles in group situations using a model of nine stereotypes, each with different behaviors. He also proposes several hypotheses referencing the basis of the roles that each of us typically occupies within a team ("Image 6. Types of roles in a group" on page 32). Belbin also gives us some important clues on the characteristics of a sustainable working group. His research postulates that, in a group of seven participants, many of the contributions are unpredictable, and that it may be difficult to bring out the opinions of certain individuals. Also, the British scholar has found that in groups with eight participants, words are circulating freely, but almost no one is listening. Groups of nine are clearly in need of a coordinator who can maintain control. With ten individuals, the coordinator has become an opinion leader, trying to impose their point of view to the detriment of others.

In conclusion, in our co-creation workshops with consumers and experts, we try to set up sessions with working groups of, at most, three or four people. At the same time, we try to have three or four groups during a session, so that everyone can present their findings, concerns, or ideas to others, with the overall result being of mutual inspiration and mutual criticism.

CO-CREATION: ON-LINE VS. OFF-LINE

The goal of this part of our guide is to analyze the difference between the co-creative process online and off-line. It should be clear that, in the latter, it is possible to involve groups of ten or twelve people at maximum, while the former offers us the opportunity to recruit hundreds of participants who can contribute to the process of co-developing an idea or a solution. In the off-line case, we refer mainly to workshops and work sessions where the number of participants is de facto limited.

We begin our analysis by assessing the main benefits of co-creation online. First, when you co-develop online, the communication tends to be more mediated: participants have more time to formulate their own response, and devote more time to re-reading and re-evaluating the contributions of others before making their own point of view. You can also use search engines to include video, sound and images in conjunction with your speech, enriching your own point of view, and providing arguments in support of your ideas, all of which can be rational, as well emotional. On the other hand, it is assumed that the participants are in their comfort zone during co-creation online. These are fundamental aspects, which ensure that everyone can work to the best of their ability. One of the pitfalls of co-creation online is the already cited the rule of 1/9/90: with statistical certainty, we can conclude that one percent of our participants generate creative ideas, nine percent sort and classify what is made from the one percent, while the vast majority of the participants will play a passive role, never becoming an active part of the discussion. Moreover, another problem concerning co-creation online lies in the multiplication of threads and sub-threads. Multiplication can shift the focus of the discussion on several issues that are not necessarily relevant to the aim of the project, as well as segment participants on the basis of their interest in a sub-discussion. It is important not to underestimate how quickly an online discussion can lose focus. Likewise, online discussion can be derailed by phones ringing, emails that arrive, family or colleagues, or even situational hazards in a public place.

The biggest benefit of co-developing in a meeting in which you partici-pate physically is the ability to challenge and criticize each other, to finally convince the other party that your ideas are, indeed, correct. In all these aspects, the body language, the tone and cadence of voice, the rhythm of the words - they play an important role. On the other hand, when you are in the same room, it is possible to stimulate, inspire and promote the creative side of each participant and to help them interact creatively: This could include a collage group, or the development of a script drawn from a film or a photo shoot. In the end, in offline operating mode, you can control the environmental conditions that stimulate the participants, for example, chairs, furniture, colors, images, and videos. It is much eas-ier to moderate the discussion, balance the groups, facilitate exchanges between participants, and identify and eliminate those participants who

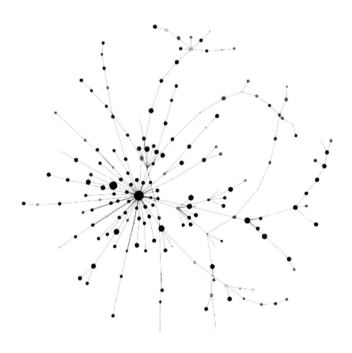

Image 7. Nesting

may be detrimental to the performance of the work of the group. Of course, there are also risks associated with co-creating off-line. First, the client assumes a passive attitude during the process, as could occur during a focus group. Instead of actively participating, some customers identify themselves as observers, not really making a personal contribution to the workshop, or trying to analyze the cause-effect relationships of the discussions that take place between the active participants. In the end, the co-creation workshop can last for seven or eight hours at a time, for one or two days in a row and are thus comparable to a marathon, where you need to balance forces in order to get to the finish line. Many people underestimate this and behave as if they were already in the sprint final, remaining powerless and silent for most of co-creation itself.

RATIONAL, IRRATIONAL AND UNREALISTIC EXPECTATIONS

Before addressing the issue of expectations in co-creation, we will do a little 'peep' into the world of Japanese design, using the example of Muji. The company was launched in Japan in 1979 as a vertical brand which offered design products for the home, office and clothing. The philosophy is that the simplicity of the lines can quickly turn 'minimalism' into an obsession. The term Muji comes from the phrase "Mujirushi Ryohin", which can be translated as "quality products without brand." At this time, Muji is known for anonymous design, creative uses of recycled materials, and the continued focus on reduction of waste materials in the production and in the packaging of their goods. Even individual products are never attributed to specific designers; Muji is considered a designer brand, and one of the icons of minimalist design. The leaders of Muji learned that their customers were enjoying the simplicity of the products, but still wished to be able to customize. Already in 2002, having understood the importance of involving their customers in a process

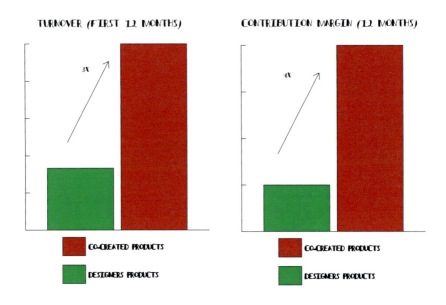

Image 8. Muji Comparison after 12 months

of co-creation, they launched a program of product co-development, selecting customers to co-create together with the designers. Customers are offered a percent of sales of the product created, assuming it were to succeed. A study at the University of Vienna and the University of Tokyo compared the economic performance of the products co-created with those of the products of traditional design, leading to surprising results.

During the first twelve months, the products which were co-created sold more than three times that of standard design products, generating a contribution margin four times higher. In the first three years after its launch, the results are even more astonishing, since the difference in the contribution margin increased to six times, and the revenues generated by co-created products were five times greater than the traditional products. Furthermore, the products, which involve co-development, have a higher likelihood of exceeding the three-year trial period, after which new products are added to the permanent catalog of Muji.

These results are important for two reasons: first of all, they reassure us that co-creation has economic benefits in the short and long term. Furthermore, Muji represents a benchmark clear, but also an asymptotic point, which may not really be possible for others to achieve. Not all companies that plunge into the world of co-creation achieve the same results as the Japanese, and it is not our intention to create expectations in this regard. Co-creation is a process that generates good results, but whose final result is still raw. Although belonging to the purists of co-creation, and having great confidence in the results of the process is our deep belief, we also know that there are variables that are beyond the capacity of the co-creators who make the products that we see in the markets. Firstly the structure of a brand, its values, its raison d'être, depend on strategic considerations and choices that can only be developed inside the company. At the same time, the vision and mission of a company reflects

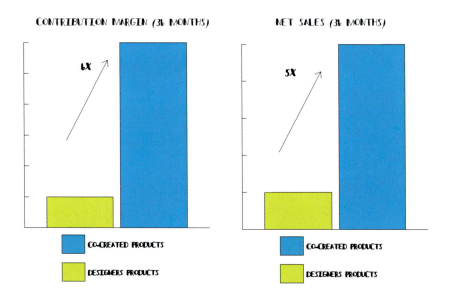

Image 9. Muji Comparison after 36 months

the leadership and culture, and cannot be disturbed by co-creation. It can be influenced, for example, by using co-creation as a litmus test that measures the relevance and uniqueness of a vision, although still reflect logic that goes well beyond the desires of customers. A clear example is the culture of a company, which reflects the leadership of those in command, internal capabilities, as well as the ownership structure. Just think of the extreme case of family businesses, in which the "culture" of the company affects the culture of the family.

These relationships can also be found in larger companies, such as Steve Jobs and Apple, Michael Dell and Dell, and Bill Gates and Microsoft. And, as well, the relationships that fashion entrepreneurs such as Prada, Armani, and Rosso have with their maisons are also excellent examples. Furthermore, there are unique characteristics of an operational establishment: the relationship between the company and suppliers, the ability to adapt to sudden changes, all of which are ideas that go well beyond the standard precepts of co-creation. In our experience co-creating with customers around the world, we have stood in front of beautiful ideas, co-generated during workshops, which never made it to market: one of the most significant reasons being confusion stemming from a lack of knowledge about how to integrate current abilities and understanding what can and cannot be done. Co-creation is designed to establish a new relationship with end users, even using them as a source of inspiration for redefining the current process. This can aid in the formation of diagnostics which allow business owners to be increasingly proactive and better understand the weaknesses and strengths of their business, ultimately allowing them to transform their ideas into viable commercial solutions.

CO-CREATING
WITH SUCCESS

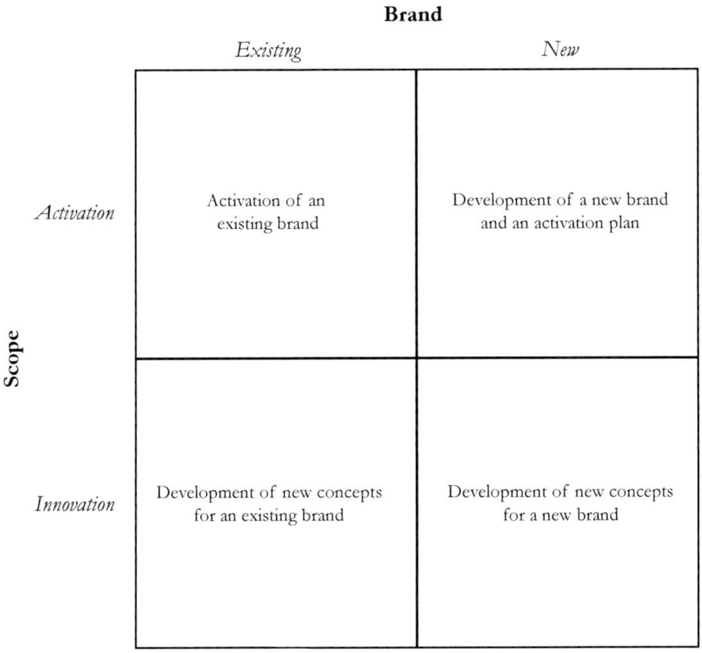

Brand

	Existing	*New*
Activation	Activation of an existing brand	Development of a new brand and an activation plan
Innovation	Development of new concepts for an existing brand	Development of new concepts for a new brand

(Scope — vertical axis label)

Image 10. Co-creation Objectives

In order to co-create with success, there are basic conditions that must be met within the company and externally. We will first examine all the internal conditions, beginning with what the company can and should control. First, it is essential to formalize the objectives and constraints of the co-creation project. These constraints often create traps. Although it is important to define which elements are included and excluded from the process, too often these decisions are not black and white. For example, there are cases in which characteristics of the brand or product you do not want to change or cannot be distorted. It often happened with producers of alcoholic and non-alcoholic beverages, who wanted to exclude the organoleptic characteristics of the product and were quite interested in developing new concepts regarding the primary and secondary packaging. In other cases, for customers within the household appliances sector, the lowest levels of brand architecture could be developed from scratch. In other situations, however, they were not part of the discussion. In the event that these objectives and constraints are not clearly stated, the result of the process is likely to become highly undesirable.

We must accurately formalize if the result of co-creation must refer back to existing brands or is designed to create new platforms or innovative products. Referring to Image 10, we postulate that there are four cases, and for the proper conduct of the trial, it is not recommended to put goals that fall at the same time in most cases. Instead, we recommend focusing on one at time. Suppose that the goal is to co-create a new tablet: it is intuitive to assume that the process of co-creation is different if the tablet is launched with a brand new design that has been co-created, rather than simply becoming part of the product portfolio, such is the case with brands including Samsung or Dell. It is often necessary to focus on one of four categories of targets, and possibly launch parallel processes that fall into another category, if the strategy requires.

Concerning the constraints and objectives, in our personal experience, problems arise at the extremes of the range, or if the objectives and constraints are too defined or, inversely, if they are too general. In the first case, you are likely to clip the wings of creativity, removing possible opportunities in favor of one short answer. In the second case, the probability that the result is of the will of the client is the same as winning the lottery, because in fact, the result of co-creation becomes unpredictable. Once the objectives are clear and formalized, it is important to select key participants within the company, those who can make a concrete contribution to the process of co-creation, and managers who have decision-making power within the project. Typically, these individuals work in marketing, sales, research and development, and market research. You need a balanced mix of various levels of hierarchy, so that the decision-makers involved know who should perform and can enjoy a better view of the field. Additionally, these individuals can help make a contribution already in the conceptual phase. In extreme cases, where participants are too junior or too senior, it is likely that co-creation will not have a strategic vision and will find itself with a lack of support for the direction, or rather lack of operability and feasibility.

Concerning the participants of the company, it should be noted that it is critical to prepare well, even if you have no prior experience. Even though there are experts in a field or industry, the process of co-creation is a process without hierarchy, which is why you have to adapt to a working group in which the opinion of experts has the same value as that of others, both internal or external. There is no bigger problem in the co-creation process than when a participant, relying on their experience and their superior level in the traditional hierarchy, uses their credentials to defend an idea that others do not like.

Concerning the external factors, two dimensions require direct attention: the profile of the participants and the environment of co-creation. In fact, you are given ample space to develop a profile of participants, but it is necessary to emphasize once again how this dimension represents one of the conditions required to obtain satisfactory results in the co-creative process. Although we have seen that it is necessary to have a certain diversity of profiles and a balanced mix, the minimum condition to deal with co-creation includes profiles which feature creativity and a critical eye. The group should at least look at existing solutions in the form of criticism, and seek solutions that are out of the ordinary.

Concerning the environment, we'll just suggest a place with plenty of natural light, plenty of space, a creative and comfortable feeling, but also discontinuous in the furnishings. The latter is an important dimension during the workshop because it can stimulate a team in trouble by simply moving them to another side of the room to work, allowing for a change of view or perspective. In the case of co-creation online, you have to organize and plan the visual stimuli consistent with the objectives of co-creation: it is assumed, in fact, that the above objectives are translated into a graphic for the web interface that is consistent with the context of co-creation.

CO-CREATION WORKSHOPS EXAMPLES

In this chapter, we examine in detail some examples of co-creation workshops conducted by the writer. Referring to picture 10 of the previous chapter, we examine four examples:

- Co-creating a platform for the activation of existing brand (Moscow, Russia)
- Co-creation of a promotional platform for the launch of a co-branding product (Amsterdam, Netherlands).
- Co-creation of new products for an existing brand (Toronto, Canada).
- Co-creation of new products for a new brand (New York, United States)

Of course, to protect the confidentiality agreements and our relationship with business clients, we will present examples without giving details about the brands, still trying to be thorough in the information proposed. As often happens in advisory, and especially in innovation projects that reach the market 2-3 years later, "talk of the sin or of the sinner, never provide details of both.".

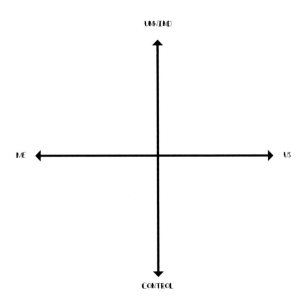

Image 11. Co-creation Excercise

1. ACTIVATION OF AN EXISTING BRAND

A multi-national company in the food sector, with a strong direct route-to-market in Russia, contacted us to define a platform for consumption in the local market, developing consumer-relevant and interesting interactions for their local consumers. In particular, on the subject of co-creation, this client represented an international brand, which, a few months prior, had changed its position by strengthening its base on the imaginary of the country of its origin. The project we have executed for the client included two distinct components. Firstly, we have analyzed and classified various opportunities for consumption for segments of the customer's objectives for the brand. As a result, we have classified the different consumption opportunities and generated lists of possible solutions that maximize potential in terms of image, volume and future growth expectations. The second phase was focused on a process of co-creation with consumer opinion leaders in the reference category of the brand in Russia.

The consumer group included adults between twenty-two and twenty-six years of age at the end of their college career and about to begin their first post-university professional experience. An important selection criterion was also their artistic propensity. In fact, each member of the group had creative hobbies, including fashion design, writing travel blogs, or playing as part of a musical group that performed regularly in Moscow. Moreover, among the participants, we've included two graphics designers, who had the job of illustrating the concepts discussed, and an expert of the Horeca channel, the presence of which was intended to demonstrate the perspective of the professional industry. The workshop also involved active participation, featuring four representatives of the client - two from international headquarters, responsible for marketing and trade marketing, and two others from the local office, responsible for sales and marketing to local consumers. For this project, we have chosen to run a workshop about eight hours in duration. The site chosen was one of many 'anti-bar' in Moscow, or creative spaces at which you pay an entry fee and have access to services (such as WI-FI) as well as various refreshments. These locations do not provide table service, and they are often used by students as a place to relax and meet friends or to work on projects, or even more often by groups that come together for role-playing games. Also, this anti-bar was located in the north-east of Moscow in a former manufacturing complex, characterized by buildings with spacious brick and burgundy colors, which now house a museum of creativity for children, and various galleries art and design shops.

We typically begin the day by introducing one another, then moving on to an exercise in which the group is divided into three units; each of which includes a balanced number of internal professionals and external customer demographics. Each team then has the task of working together to develop a creative map of the brand in question. In this case, we asked the participants to cut out parts of magazines and brand images and place them on a map specially defined for the purpose. We also asked participants to identify areas of collages that were more relevant to their experience with the specific brand and the category in general. In the end, each team presents its collage to the other in an attempt to offer inspiration and mutual feedback, as well as enrich and expand the points of view of all participants. This stage of co-creation has two basic goals: to help the group to think creatively, giving all the opportunity to explore their creative potential, and also to place each individual with a group of people with whom they have never interacted before, creating a dynamic environment.

This also allows all participants to share their point of view on the brand in question and then share a common starting point in the journey of

Image 12. Example of a Co-creation Map

co-creation. Although it was not necessarily the case in this project, due to recent repositioning of brand, this stage typically involves a diagnostic assessment of the brand and the opportunity to make quality assessments in absolute terms and relative to direct competitors.

Ultimately, on both the analytical and the creative level, we have passed the stage of development for new ideas. This stage of co-creation was also divided into two parts: the first being development, and the second focused on the launch of the same product in the local market.

As planned, the group was divided into three teams, and each was assigned a task to work on. In addition, we provided each group with a document that included guidelines and worksheets to fill out, which forced the group to seek consensus, and served to formalize the ideas in black and white. Also, graphic designers have rotated among the groups to help visualize ideas immediately, so as to provide a tool not only for the subsequent presentation of each team, but also to foster greater discussion within each sub-group.

As before, ideas generated at the end of each stage of teamwork were shown in presentation, and the reactions of all participants were documented and explored. At the end of eight hours of co-creation, the group of exhausted but excited participants has devised three concepts which were very creative and relevant from a point of view of the final consumer. We also learned a lot about the forms of consumption of brands and products in Russia, as well as the preferences among young Russians for domestic and foreign brands.

2. CO–BRANDING PROMOTIONAL PLATFORM

This project was one of the most difficult of our professional career. Two big brands in the high technology industry tasked us to co-develop a professional platform for the launch of a product line in co-branding. Part of the challenge stemmed primarily from the combination of the two brands, the first of which was a historical undertaking from the hardware perspective, the second being a brand new endeavor. The difference in corporate culture was also very striking: the first organization invested in market research, and evaluated, validated and tested new products before making a decision, while the second tested new attributes and characteristics of software through changes 'in production', hoping to determine whether or not it was valid in the real market without spending time and money in brand architectures, which at the time, made it ill-suited to share the stage with the other brand. At the request of the costumer, we invited the hardware manufacturer, experts in co-creation from Amsterdam, as well as participants from around the world, including technology experts from Israel, French Telecom experts, German think tank analysts, entrepreneurs from Barcelona, local and industrial designers from Singapore, as well as experts in the internet industry operating in Silicon Valley.

In fact, the choice of Amsterdam was strategic from a logistical point of view, because all the participants were able to fly directly to the Dutch city, while other European cities would require more extensive travel. Furthermore, Amsterdam is a city where the tradition of the past and the uncertainty of the future are combined to form a balanced and creative framework for our project.

The seat of our co-creation in Amsterdam was a loft located in the north of the city from the shore opposite the river IJ, reached via ferries which departed regularly from the famous central railway station of the city, The loft, pictured above, was furnished in minimalist shape but was very functional, containing large windows overlooking the river IJ and the platforms used for loading and unloading goods at the port of Amsterdam. The external participants were joined by representatives of the companies in question, whose roles included marketing, sales, research and development, among others.

The workshop was unusual due to the number of participants involved, and lasted about six hours. Following a brief introduction of each participant, we switched to creative discussion, where the group was divided into smaller teams, and each was asked to discuss and present three global trends of great impact from the point of view of consumers. Each of these groups also presented an example of each trend, as well as the impact it could have on each of the brands involved in the project.

After completion of the presentation of the trends and after a brief sharing of reactions, we moved on to the next stage, in which those responsible for research and development in the two companies introduced the product line, showing prototypes, and listing them according to their opportunities and threats. After a brief discussion served to clarify some aspects of these products, which was useful in helping participants digest the new information, we again split the group into smaller teams, each tasked to formulate a strategy for the launch of each product, focusing especially on a platform which was globally relevant. As always, we provide participants with questionnaires and guidelines to streamline team discussions, and to ensure that we can complete the project as planned. Of the five co-created platforms introduced during our workshop, two have been used in the launch of products: one to create notoriety and help provide credibility to the products with the leaders of opinion, the second as a platform for mass distribution. From the discussion were born ideas of new products, which were subsequently launched and achieved excellent results on a commercial and economic level.

3. PRODUCT INNOVATION FOR EXISTING BRAND

An international drink brand, already present in the Canadian market, and with a very localized presence in the Province of Ontario, asked for help to conceive new product ideas to be introduced in the Toronto area. Although already known by the Canadian consumers, the brand did not enjoy premium perception, and therefore the objectives of the project included the launch of products that could also improve perception while increasing opportunities for consumption and growth expectations.

In the Distillery District of Toronto, an area recently becoming host to many fashion designers boutiques, restaurants, bars and art galleries, we had four hours available for a group of ten young people between twenty-five and thirty years, each of which had experience in fashion, advertising and publishing. This was largely thanks to the PR Agency of the brand, which has helped us to get in touch with a group of local opinion leaders. Most importantly, these individuals were Canadian.

Brand representatives responsible for the marketing and sales channel in Canada, as well as the director of customer relations, attended the meeting. After a brief introduction on the brand, we divided the group into three teams and asked each of them to describe through pictures and a map - similar to Image 12 - their perception of the image and their perception of the brand. At the end of this first phase (Image 13), it was clear that the challenge of the brand went beyond that provided by the head of marketing. In fact, among the comments given, one continues to resonate:

> *"When I go to an event and I give away a bottle of your product it is normal for me to accept it, because it's free. But why do you think that will convince me to buy your brand?"*

In fact, this, along with other comments, made it clear that the marketing strategy and the business existed in contradiction to one another. On the

Image 13. Brand Maps Toronto

one hand, it was a premium brand in the media, but also featured poor quality at the point of sale. On the other hand, the brand enjoyed aggressive penetration of the Horeca channel, but their promotional strategy for reducing prices in supermarkets and appealing to general consumers was far too aggressive.

This was, of course, a barrier to entry for many, and generated far too much confusion for all consumers. In the second and third stage of this process of co-creation, we decided to take advantage of the efficiency of the teams that managed to churn out new ideas by performing a change in the course of work. Instead of the initial concept for the team, the groups churned out three concepts, the first one that was relevant to the group itself and designed to convince others to enter the world of the brand and buy the products; the second, on the contrary, involved them finally moving away from the brand and the product, identifying what to do and, simultaneously, all that was to be avoided.

In the light of what had transpired during the workshop, sales management and marketing professionals of the brand saw fit to change the current strategy of activation and modify expansion plans for other provinces of Canada. In addition, two of the concepts created during co-creation were launched in the market with excellent commercial results and visibility.

4. PRODUCT INNOVATION FOR NEW BRAND

In the heart of the Big Apple, not far from the center of Manhattan, we performed a series of three mini co-creations, with the aim of enriching the product concepts and prototypes for a manufacturer of devices for personal well-being. The client company was working on a long project to launch a new brand for the elderly, and at the same time evaluating the product portfolio by launching exclusively within the same demographic. The objective of co-creation was two-fold: the first task – with the challenge presented exclusively from the side of the product and not the brand – was to evaluate and enrich product ideas so that they might be based on clear information and relevant to the needs of consumers. The products needed to be perceived as innovative and credible at the same time. Moreover, the goal of the process was to enrich these concepts, and evaluate prototypes so that there was a difference between the expectations created by the concept and the performance and functionality of the prototype itself. The process of co-creation took place over two days, including three mini sessions of four hours each. Each session was attended by one to three representatives of the client company, a graphic designer, and, six to seven consumer opinion leaders. Each session focused on a specific category of products, prompting consumers to choose among the various categories, but allowing for in-depth research of each line of products.

In each session, after a brief introduction of the participants and a rapid warm-up exercise, one of the representatives of the company read the concept describing the product line, and then answered various questions while providing further clarification to all participants. For those who do not have relevant experience, a concept has a fairly standardized form, and includes three sections, which, are referred to as: actual consumer belief, benefits, and the reason to believe. The first is nothing more than a variation of the needs of the consumer, and to be clear, is that part translated into traditional advertising in the initial phase of the ad, or when the mother of the child compares the faded T-shirt with that friend. The second is represented only by juxtaposing the offer of the brand, the product, or the benefits, with the uniqueness of the offering. The third part is the one driving credibility, which fuels whether consumers believe the expectations generated by the first two elements of the concept: it can often be attributed to the shape of the product or the packaging, such as a liquid detergent rather than powder, or multicolored toothpaste rather than one with a single, unique color. In the end, in their traditional form, the concepts do not include images and visualizations, but only a description.

Once all issues were clarified, we divided the group into two teams, one for consumers, the other without consumers. Each team was given the task of enriching and displaying, with the help of a graphic designer, the concept described above, before presenting it to all the other participants. In this way, we collected insightful views without poisoning consumers with prototypes, and simultaneously giving them an opportunity to generate new and fresh ideas, new forms and new points of view. Once each team had finished and presented to the others, we introduced the prototypes in the groups, by demonstrating their operation. We then asked them to repeat the same process from the previous year. In this way, we were able to verify that the expectations generated by the concepts were more or less anticipated, ranging from the physical form and technical characteristics of the prototypes to consumer opinion on the modus operandi of the line products. The process of co-creation has allowed us to radically change development strategies of two of the three product lines, helping to bring in new and innovative solutions which had, previously, not been utilized. Regarding the third product line, the work completed in co-creation has allowed us to reduce development time by several months.

CONCLUSIONS

Co-creation is definitely a vast and complicated concept, which means that each company involved can find a way to co-create in a manner that suits them best. But, at the same time, it is certainly true that co-creation is not for everyone. Companies that rely on creative vision and who choose to impose their way of being, no matter what may be the opinion of final consumers, are companies in which co-creation could be discounted by the values and essence of the brand. It is also true that it is not correct to generalize because we have seen the results of Muji, and we can relate the example of the fashion designer Oscar de la Renta, who used co-creation to prepare collections.

For those companies who do wish to co-create, we will examine three cases which, in our opinion, have helped lead to the co-creation of new ideas in a more expedient and relevant manner: innovation, branding and international expansion.

CO—CREATION AND INNOVATION

Co-creation is an important tool for innovation. In fact, co-creation can be used at any stage of the innovation process. You can co-create upstream, identifying known consumers and customers insights that are unique and relevant. You can also use co-creation to better understand the needs of consumers. Co-creation is a series of creative and analytical phases, so it can be easily interpolated with work sessions whose purpose is to get answers in a metaphorical fashion, which can later be decrypted in order to verify the requirements, drivers and the modus operandi of consumers.

Also, you can co-create to generate new ideas for products, services or benefits, and, in some cases, new ecosystems. Once you have a clear idea of market needs, as well as local and global trends, we can use the process of co-creation to generate ideas, experiences, new product features or new applications.

Co-creation becomes particularly useful due to the fact consumers are not bound by the terms of a determined category, which often limits the vision of a product manager or brand manager. On the other hand, you can use co-creation on an innovative concept, to enrich existing development in a way that is more relevant to consumers. In a sense, this represents the form of use and the keystone in the success of Muji: maintaining a clear vision on what products should be launched in the market, understanding the key brand philosophy, and enriching the business using an international perspective; co-creation can also ensure the quality of internal logic dictating the construction of prototypes of the product, and, ultimately, improve the project, during the final stages of development. In fact co-creation can be a worthy substitute for market research, allowing not only a diagnostic phase, but also an improvement of the product itself. And finally, co-creation can be used to devise or enrich the launch phase of the new products, improving on the effectiveness of the activities and identifying potential barriers quickly, before entering the market.

CO—CREATION AND BRANDING

The process of co-creation is typically like a funnel, where we start with more general ideas and, gradually, become more specific. Taking into account this metaphorical representation of co-creation, we can therefore say that it is possible to use co-creation to understand what threats and opportunities may exist for a brand.

Obviously in this phase, the work undertaken by the group will almost exclusively be based on a creative point of view which is less analytical and devoid of more diagnostic measurements, such as awareness, recognition, penetration, and so on. Rather, a qualitative diagnostic will be formed based on the perception of the participants and arising from the same brand, derived from existing products, advertising campaigns, social media presence (or lack of presence), promotional activities and price. In any case, it should also be noted that the results of said diagnosis, represent a working hypothesis, which must then be tested thoroughly. The process of co-creation can be used to develop powerful platforms for activation that are relevant to targeted consumers.

In this context, the process helps to answer a variety of questions, including which platform should be employed, and in what form action should be taken so that it stays relevant to the brand, the consumer, and the platform itself.

For example, take into consideration the culinary platform. You can choose from various directions, such as traditional, ethnic, fusion, and molecular cuisine. The country of origin, the chefs, the mode of activation – all are dimensions that have a strong impact on the brand, and whose relevance with consumers can be promoted by the co-creation of a powerful solution.

Co-creation can also be used in the design phase of a new brand, in order to ensure the uniqueness and relevance of it to the consumers and the market in which they are located, Often, we forget that thousands of consumers are exposed to messages from brands surrounding it, even if they are direct competitors or indirect competitors.

CO–CREATION AND INTERNATIONAL EXPANSION

In the case of international expansion, co-creation has proven to be a useful tool and acts as a catalyst. Ultimately, co-creation increases the rate of a chemical reaction without altering the final result. In cases like this, we always try to use not only consumers, but also experts in media, communication, trade, and all who will have the task of prescribing and promoting the brand. In this way, we tend to avoid missteps both from the point of view of culture and tradition, as well as from the point of view of the local market nuances. For example, in Italy, concrete restrictions may make it difficult to advertise alcoholic beverages through traditional media. In a country like Poland, it is not possible and all promotional activities are limited to the Horeca channel or retail spaces, to which access is prohibited to those who do not meet legal minimum age for consumption of these products. Then, from the point of view of an Italian producer who wants to launch their own brands and its products in Poland, a process of co-creation with consumers and experts is essential for understanding the local customs and traditions so that they can identify opportunities and threats, learn the rules of the game and legal constraints, and generate ideas on local platforms for the development of the brand. Everything becomes even more important when the physical distribution must be executed by a third party: in fact, co-creation can be used to identify what characteristics are critical for choosing the correct distribution partner in the local market.

CO—CREATION: A CHECKLIST

For those who, at the end of this short journey, enjoy the process of co-creation, this final section provides an essential quick-start guide. By invoking the definition previously given in the first chapters of this paper, we develop checklists to clarify any internal conflict with external partners, including issues related to the objectives and the purpose of co-creation. In the tablets below we propose that the following elements should to be taken into account. The list allows readers to do an "audit" of the objectives of the co-creation using the matrix presented here:.

Scope	Brand: *Existing*	Brand: *New*
Activation	Activation of an existing brand	Development of a new brand and an activation plan
Innovation	Development of new concepts for an existing brand	Development of new concepts for a new brand

Actors

Internal		**External**	
Marketing	☐	Target Mass	☐
Market Research	☐	Leader of opinion	☐
Research and Development	☐	Expert	☐
Sales	☐	Other -	☐
Other	☐		

Number of Participants

<15	☐	between 15 & 30	☐
> 30	☐		

Origin

Same country	☐	More countries	☐

Action And Object

Action		Object	
Action		**Object**	
Design	☐	Functional Characteristics	☐
Evaluate	☐	Emotional Characteristics	☐
Validate	☐	Product/ Service Usage	☐
Research	☐	Technological Innovation	☐
Other_____	☐	Innovation Ecosystem	☐
		Activation	☐
		Services	☐

Mode

On-line ☐   Off-line ☐   Mixed ☐

Our goals are not limited to only one of the four quadrants, so we highly recommend that individuals should check their own priorities, reducing the scope for one or two quadrants. We do not recommend situations involving more than two processes of co-creation in parallel in the same strategic area, where results can be in conflict. If you choose two processes in parallel, please ensure that each has its objectives centered in one quadrant.

ANNEX

REFERENCES

Achrol, R.S., Kotler, P., 2011. Frontiers of the marketing paradigm in the third millennium. J. Acad. Mark. Sci. 40, 35–52. doi:10.1007/s11747-011-0255-4

Andreu, L., Sánchez, I., Mele, C., 2010. Value co-creation among retailers and consumers: New insights into the furniture market. J. Retail. Consum. Serv. 17, 241–250. doi:10.1016/j.jretconser.2010.02.001

Baron, S., Warnaby, G., 2011. Individual customers' use and integration of resources: Empirical findings and organizational implications in the context of value co-creation. Ind. Mark. Manag. 40, 211–218. doi:10.1016/j.indmarman.2010.06.033

Belbin, R.M., 2010. Team roles at work. Routledge.

Belbin, R.M.M., 2012. Management teams. Routledge.

Bendapudi, N., Leone, R.P., 2003. Psychological implications of customer participation in co-production. J. Mark. 14–28.

Biggemann, S., Kowalkowski, C., Maley, J., Brege, S., 2013. Development and implementation of customer solutions: A study of process dynamics and market shaping. Ind. Mark. Manag. 42, 1083–1092. doi:10.1016/j.indmarman.2013.07.026

Bonabeau, E., Dorigo, M., Theraulaz, G., 1999. Swarm intelligence: from natural to artificial systems. Oxford university press New York.

Chandra, Y., Coviello, N., 2010. Broadening the concept of international entrepreneurship: "Consumers as International Entrepreneurs". J. World Bus. 45, 228–236. doi:10.1016/j.jwb.2009.09.006

Chathoth, P., Altinay, L., Harrington, R.J., Okumus, F., Chan, E.S.W., 2013. Co-production versus co-creation: A process based continuum in the hotel service context. Int. J. Hosp. Manag. 32, 11–20. doi:10.1016/j.ijhm.2012.03.009

Cherif, H., Miled, B., 2013. Are Brand Communities Influencing Brands through Co-creation? A Cross-National Example of the Brand AXE: In France and in Tunisia. Int. Bus. Res. 6. doi:10.5539/ibr.v6n9p14

Choi, J.N., Moon, W.J., 2013. Multiple Forms of Innovation Implementation. Organ. Dyn. 42, 290–297. doi:10.1016/j.orgdyn.2013.07.007

Cova, B., Salle, R., 2008. Marketing solutions in accordance with the S-D logic: Co-creating value with customer network actors. Ind. Mark. Manag. 37, 270–277. doi:10.1016/j.indmarman.2007.07.005

Enz, M.G., Lambert, D.M., 2012. Using cross-functional, cross-firm teams to co-create value: The role of financial measures. Ind. Mark. Manag. 41, 495–507. doi:10.1016/j.indmarman.2011.06.041

Feller, J., Finnegan, P., Hayes, J., O'Reilly, P., 2009. Institutionalising information asymmetry: governance structures for open innovation. Inf. Technol. People 22, 297–316. doi:http://dx.doi.org/10.1108/09593840911002423

Fournier, S., Avery, J., 2011. The uninvited brand. Bus. Horiz. 54, 193–207. doi:10.1016/j.bushor.2011.01.001

Franke, N., Schreier, M., 2007. Product uniqueness as a driver of customer utility in mass customization. Mark. Lett. 19, 93–107. doi:10.1007/s11002-007-9029-7

Gebauer, J., Füller, J., Pezzei, R., 2013. The dark and the bright side of co-creation: Triggers of member behavior in online innovation communities. J. Bus. Res. 66, 1516–1527. doi:10.1016/j.jbusres.2012.09.013

Grissemann, U.S., Stokburger-Sauer, N.E., 2012. Customer co-creation of travel services: The role of company support and customer satisfaction with the co-creation performance. Tour. Manag. 33, 1483–1492. doi:10.1016/j.tourman.2012.02.002

Gyrd-Jones, R.I., Kornum, N., 2013. Managing the co-created brand: Value and cultural complementarity in online and offline multi-stakeholder ecosystems. J. Bus. Res. 66, 1484–1493. doi:10.1016/j.jbusres.2012.02.045

Haaranen, T., Nisar, T.M., 2011. Innovative ways of raising funds and adding value: A stakeholder approach to whole business securitization. Bus. Horiz. 54, 457–466. doi:10.1016/j.bushor.2011.05.001

Ind, N., Iglesias, O., Schultz, M., 2013. Building Brands Together.

Calif. Manage. Rev. 55.

Kohler, T., Fueller, J., Matzler, K., Stieger, D., 2011. Co-creation in virtual worlds: The design of the user experience. MIS Q. 35, 773–788.

Kohler, T., Matzler, K., Füller, J., 2009. Avatar-based innovation: Using virtual worlds for real-world innovation. Technovation 29, 395–407. doi:10.1016/j.technovation.2008.11.004

Kohtamäki, M., Partanen, J., Möller, K., 2013. Making a profit with R&D services — The critical role of relational capital. Ind. Mark. Manag. 42, 71–81. doi:10.1016/j. indmarman.2012.11.001

Kuppelwieser, V.G., Simpson, M.C., Chiummo, G., 2013. 1 + 1 does not always equal value creation: The case of YouTube. Mark. Lett. 24, 311–321. doi:10.1007/s11002-013-9246-1

Lamberti, L., Noci, G., 2009. Online experience as a lever of customer involvement in NPD: An exploratory analysis and a research agenda. EuroMed J. Bus. 4, 69–87. doi:10.1108/14502190910956701

Lang, K.R., Shang, R.D., Vragov, R., 2009. Designing markets for co-production of digital culture goods. Decis. Support Syst. 48, 33–45. doi:10.1016/j.dss.2009.05.010

Lang, K.R., Walden, E.A., 2009. Introduction to the special section on information product markets. Decis. Support Syst. 48, 1–2. doi:10.1016/j.dss.2009.05.004

Lee, S.M., Olson, D.L., Trimi, S., 2012. Co-innovation: convergenomics, collaboration, and co-creation for organizational values. Manag. Decis. 50, 817–831. doi:10.1108/00251741211227528

Lehrer, M., Ordanini, A., DeFillippi, R., Miozzo, M., 2012. Challenging the orthodoxy of value co-creation theory: A contingent view of co-production in design-intensive business services. Eur. Manag. J. 30, 499–509. doi:10.1016/j.emj.2012.07.006

McPherson, M., Smith-Lovin, L., Cook, J.M., 2001. Birds of a Feather: Homophily in Social Networks. Annu. Rev. Sociol. 27, 415–444. doi:10.1146/annurev.soc.27.1.415

Mele, C., 2011. Conflicts and value co-creation in project networks. Ind. Mark. Manag. 40, 1377–1385. doi:10.1016/j. indmarman.2011.06.033

Mitleton-Kelly, E., 2003. Ten principles of complexity and enabling infrastructures. Elsevier.

Mochon, D., Norton, M.I., Ariely, D., 2012. Bolstering and restoring feelings of competence via the IKEA effect. Int. J. Res. Mark. 29, 363–369. doi:10.1016/j.ijresmar.2012.05.001

Muñiz, A.M., Schau, H.J., 2011. How to inspire value-laden collaborative consumer-generated content. Bus. Horiz. 54, 209–217. doi:10.1016/j.bushor.2011.01.002

Nishikawa, H., Schreier, M., Ogawa, S., 2013. User-generated versus designer-generated products: A performance assessment at Muji. Int. J. Res. Mark. 30, 160–167. doi:10.1016/j.ijresmar.2012.09.002

Nuttavuthisit, K., 2010. If you can't beat them, let them join: The development of strategies to foster consumers' co-creative practices. Bus. Horiz. 53, 315–324. doi:10.1016/j.bushor.2010.01.005

OHern, M.S., Rindfleisch, A., 2010. Customer Co-Creation: A Typology and Research Agenda. Rev. Mark. Res. 6, 84–106. doi:10.1108/S1548-6435(2009)0000006008

Payne, A., Storbacka, K., Frow, P., Knox, S., 2009. Co-creating brands: Diagnosing and designing the relationship experience. J. Bus. Res. 62, 379–389. doi:10.1016/j.jbusres.2008.05.013

Prahalad, C.K., Ramaswamy, V., 2000. Co-opting Customer Competence. Harv. Bus. Rev. 78, 79–87.

Song, J.H., Adams, C.R., 1993. Differentiation through Customer Involvement in Production or Delivery. J. Consum. Mark. 10, 4–12.

Tynan, C., McKechnie, S., Chhuon, C., 2010. Co-creating value for luxury brands. J. Bus. Res. 63, 1156–1163. doi:10.1016/j.jbusres.2009.10.012

Vallaster, C., von Wallpach, S., 2013. An online discursive inquiry into the social dynamics of multi-stakeholder brand meaning co-creation. J. Bus. Res. 66, 1505–1515. doi:10.1016/j.jbusres.2012.09.012

Vernette, E., Hamdi-Kidar, L., 2013. Co-creation with consumers : who has the competence and wants to cooperate. Int. J. Mark. Res. 55, 539–561.

Wang, Y., Li, D., 2013. Testing the moderating effects of toolkits and user communities in personalization: The case of social networking service. Decis. Support Syst. 55, 31–42. doi:10.1016/j.dss.2012.12.045

Yi, Y., Gong, T., 2013. Customer value co-creation behavior: Scale development and validation. J. Bus. Res. 66, 1279–1284. doi:10.1016/j.jbusres.2012.02.026

Zhang, X., Chen, R., 2008. Examining the mechanism of the value co-creation with customers. Int. J. Prod. Econ. 116, 242–250. doi:10.1016/j.ijpe.2008.09.004

Zhang, X., Ye, C., Chen, R., Wang, Z., 2011. Multi-focused strategy in value co-creation with customers: Examining cumulative development pattern with new capabilities. Int. J. Prod. Econ. 132, 122–130. doi:10.1016/j.ijpe.2011.03.019

TABLE OF IMAGES

INDEX

Filiberto Amati was born in Naples in 1974. After earning a bachelor's degree in engineering management from the University of Naples Federico II, moved to Belgium, where he worked for three years at the Brussels headquarters of Procter & Gamble. At the end of this work experience, he changed his residence to Barcelona, where he obtained an MBA from IESE Business School.

Filiberto then moved to Amsterdam, where he worked first for Auberon, a small consulting company, and subsequently, ad-interim for the consumer electronics division of Philips. Later, he joined the Gruppo Campari, for which he traveled the world, working in destinations such as southern France, the Caribbean, Mexico, and Belgium. His adventure continued in 2012 in Warsaw, where he opened his own consulting firm, Amati & Associates, and where he is attending a PhD program at INE PAN, the Institute of Economics of the Polish Academy of Sciences.

Made in the USA
Monee, IL
01 January 2021